HOUGHTON MIFFLIN
math
CENTRAL

D1407009

One
Two

Buckle My Shoe

Poems, Rhymes, Songs and Chants for Math

HOUGHTON MIFFLIN

Boston • Atlanta • Dallas • Geneva, Illinois • Princeton, New Jersey • Palo Alto

Acknowledgments

Grateful acknowledgment is made for permission to reprint original or copyrighted materials as follows:

"Animals' Houses" from *Complete Poems for Children* by James Reeves (Heinemann). Copyright © James Reeves. Reprinted by permission of the James Reeves Estate.

"The Ants at the Olympics" from *Animal Alphabet* by Richard Digance. Published by Michael Joseph Ltd.

"Barney Has a Basketball" from *Move Over Mother Goose* by Ruth I. Dowell. Copyright ©1987 by Ruth I. Dowell. Reprinted with permission of the publisher, Gryphon House, Inc., Beltsville, MD 20704.

"Bedtime" from *Silver Sand and Snow* by Eleanor Farjeon. Reprinted by permission of David Higham Associates Ltd.

"Behind the Museum Door" from *Good Rhymes, Good Times* by Lee Bennett Hopkins. Copyright ©1973, 1995 by Lee Bennett Hopkins. Reprinted by permission of Curtis Brown, Ltd.

"The Black Pebble" from *Complete Poems for Children* by James Reeves (Heinemann). Copyright © James Reeves. Reprinted by permission of the James Reeves Estate.

"Brachiosaurus" from *Yellow Butter Purple Jelly Red Jam Black Bread* by Mary Ann Hoberman. Copyright ©1981 by Mary Ann Hoberman. Reprinted by permission of Gina Maccoby Literary Agency.

"Bugs" by Margaret Wise Brown. Reprinted by permission of the author.

"Centipede" from *One at a Time* by David McCord. Copyright ©1974 by David McCord. By permission of Little, Brown and Company.

"Charley Needs a Haircut" from *Move Over Mother Goose* by Ruth I. Dowell. Copyright ©1987 by Ruth I. Dowell. Reprinted with permission of the publisher, Gryphon House, Inc., Beltsville, MD 20704.

"Circles" from *The Little Hill: Poems & Pictures* by Harry Behn. Copyright 1949 by Harry Behn. Copyright renewed 1977 by Alice L. Behn. By permission of Marian Reiner.

"Counting Petals" from *Cricket in a Thicket* by Aileen Fisher. Copyright ©1963 by Aileen Fisher. By permission of the author, Aileen Fisher, who controls rights.

"Dangerous" from *All Together* by Dorothy Aldis. Copyright 1925-1928, 1934, 1939, 1952, © renewed 1953-1956, 1962, 1967 by Dorothy Aldis. Reprinted by permission of G. P. Putnam's Sons.

"Dividing" from *One at a Time* by David McCord. Copyright ©1952 by David McCord. By permission of Little, Brown and Company.

"East and West" from *Finger Frolics* compiled by Liz Cromwell and Dixie Hibner. Copyright ©1976 by Partner Press. Reprinted by permission of Gryphon House, Inc., Beltsville, MD 20704.

"Eight Pigs" from *Finger Frolics* compiled by Liz Cromwell and Dixie Hibner. Copyright ©1976 by Partner Press. Reprinted by permission of Gryphon House, Inc., Beltsville, MD 20704.

"Every Time I Climb a Tree" from *One at a Time* by David McCord. Copyright ©1952 by David McCord. By permission of Little, Brown and Company.

"Feet" from *Cricket in a Thicket* by Aileen Fisher. Copyright ©1963 by Aileen Fisher. By permission of the author, Aileen Fisher, who controls rights.

"A Few Is Not So Many" from *Move Over Mother Goose* by Ruth I. Dowell. Copyright ©1987 by Ruth I. Dowell. Reprinted with permission of the publisher, Gryphon House, Inc., Beltsville, MD 20704.

"Fishes' Evening Song" from *Whisperings and Other Things* by Dahlov Ipcar. Copyright ©1967 by Dahlov Ipcar. Published by Knopf, Random House. Reprinted by permission of McIntosh & Otis, Inc.

"Follow the Leader" from *The Wizard in the Well: Poems & Pictures* by Harry Behn. Copyright ©1956 by Harry Behn. Copyright renewed 1984 by Alice Behn Goebel, Pamela Behn Adam, Peter Behn, and Prescott Behn. Used by permission of Marian Reiner.

"How Do You Make a Pizza Grow?" from *Blackberry Ink* by Eve Merriam. Copyright ©1985 by Eve Merriam. Reprinted by permission of Marian Reiner.

(continued on page 125)

Using *One, Two, Buckle My Shoe*

The selections in *One, Two, Buckle My Shoe* are organized by math strand: Counting, Addition and Subtraction, Place Value, Time and Money, Geometry and Fractions, Measurement, and Multiplication and Division. This chart correlates the literature selections in the Anthology to each chapter theme in Grades 1 and 2. Stars (★) indicate Chapter Opener selections. Cross-referenced entries indicate suggestions for additional uses of each selection.

MATH STRAND	SELECTION	PAGE	GRADE 1	GRADE 2
Counting *Strand for:* Grade 1: Chapter 1 Grade 2: Chapter 1	**Ten Little Froggies** *Louise Binder Scott*	2	★ Chapter 1 Chapter 9	Chapter 12
	Treasure *Lee Bennett Hopkins*	4	Chapter 5	★ Chapter 1
	Counting Song *Mexican Folk Song*	6	Chapter 1	Chapter 5
	Winter Clothes *Karla Kuskin*	8	Chapter 3	Chapter 5
	Five Little Chickadees *American Counting Song*	10	Chapter 9	Chapter 8
	Over in the Meadow *Traditional*	12	Chapter 3 Chapter 9	Chapter 12
	Hurry, Little Pony *Spanish Folk Song*	14	Chapter 3 Chapter 11	Chapter 9
	This Old Man *English Folk Song*	16	Chapter 5 Chapter 11	Chapter 2
	The Black Pebble *James Reeves*	18	Chapter 5 Chapter 10	Chapter 1 Chapter 4
	Counting Petals *Aileen Fisher*	19	Chapter 3	Chapter 10
	In the Cupboard *Barbara Ireson*	20	Chapter 2 Chapter 7	Chapter 1 Chapter 10
	A Few Is Not So Many *Ruth I. Dowell*	21	Chapter 11	Chapter 2
	Oliver Twist *Traditional*	22	Chapter 12	Chapter 2 Chapter 9

USING ONE, TWO, BUCKLE MY SHOE

Ten Little Froggies

by Louise Binder Scott

Ten little froggies were swimming in a pool.

This little froggie said, "Let's go to school!"

This little froggie said, "Oh yes! Let's go!"

This little froggie said, "We'll sit in a row."

This little froggie said, "We'll learn to read."

This little froggie said, "Yes, yes indeed."

This little froggie said, "We'll learn to write."

This little froggie said, "We'll try with all our might."

This little froggie said, "We'll draw and sing."

This little froggie said, "We'll learn EVERYTHING!"

We'll come back here and swim in our pool.

Treasure

by Lee Bennett Hopkins

A rusty door key,

A part of a tool,

A dead bee I was saving

   to take in to school;

A crust of pizza,

Sand from the shore,

A piece of lead pipe,

An old apple core;

My library card,

A small model rocket —

I guess
it
is
time

to
clean
out
my
pocket.

Counting Song

Mexican Folk Song

Uno, dos y tres,

cuatro, cinco, seis,

siete, ocho,

nueve, y ahora diez.

La la la la la.

Counting Song

Mexican Folk Song

U - no, dos y tres,

cua - tro, cin - co, seis, sie - te, o - cho,

nue - ve, y a - hor - a diez.

La la la la la la la la la la la la la la la

la. la la la la la la.

Winter Clothes

by Karla Kuskin

Under my hood I have a hat

And under that

My hair is flat.

Under my coat

My sweater's blue.

My sweater's red.

I'm wearing two.

My muffler muffles to my chin

And round my neck

And then tucks in.

My gloves were knitted

By my aunts.

I've mittens too

And pants

And pants

And boots

And shoes

With socks inside.

The boots are rubber, red and wide.

And when I walk

I must not fall

Because I can't get up at all.

Five Little Chickadees

American Counting Song

Five little chickadees peeping at the door,
One flew away and then there were four;
CHORUS   Chickadee, chickadee, happy and gay,
Chickadee, chickadee, fly away.

Four little chickadees sitting on a tree,
One flew away and then there were three;
CHORUS

Three little chickadees looking at you,
One flew away and then there were two;
CHORUS

Two little chickadees sitting in the sun,
One flew away and then there was one;
CHORUS

One little chickadee left all alone,
It flew away and then there were none;
CHORUS

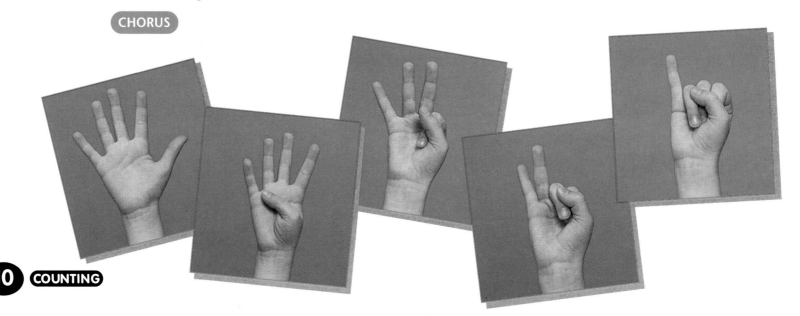

Five Little Chickadees

American Counting Song

Lightly

Verse | G | C | D7

Five lit-tle chick-a-dees peep-ing at the door, One flew a-

G

CHORUS

way and then there were four; Chick-a-dee, chick-a-dee,

G   D7   G

hap-py and gay, Chick-a-dee, chick-a-dee, fly a - way.

Over in the Meadow

Traditional

Over in the meadow in the sand in the sun,
Lived Old Mother Turtle and her little turtle one.
"Wink," said his mother. "I wink," said the one.
So they winked and they blinked in the sand in the sun.

Over in the meadow where the stream runs through,
Lived Old Mother Fish and her little fishes two.
"Swim," said their mother. "We swim," said the two.
So they swam all day where the stream runs through.

Over in the meadow in a hole in a tree,
Lived Old Mother Owl and her little owlets three.
"Hoot," said their mother. "We hoot," said the three.
So they hooted all day in the hole in the tree.

Over in the meadow, 'neath the old barn floor,
Lived Old Mother Mouse and her little mice four.
"Scamper," said their mother. "We scamper," said the four.
So they scampered all day 'neath the old barn floor.

Over in the meadow in a big beehive,
Lived Old Mother Bee and her little bees five.
"Hum," said their mother. "We hum," said the five.
So they hummed all day 'round the big beehive.

Over in the meadow in a nest built of sticks,
Lived Old Mother Raven and her little ravens six.
"Croak," said their mother. "We croak," said the six.
So they croaked all day in the nest built of sticks.

Over in the meadow where the land lies so even,
Lived Old Mother Toad and her little toads seven.
"Hop," said their mother. "We hop," said the seven.
So they hopped all day where the land lies so even.

Over in the meadow by an old mossy gate,
Lived Old Mother Possum and her little possums eight.
"Play possum," said their mother. "We play," said the eight.
So they possumed all day by the old mossy gate.

Over in the meadow near a loblolly pine,
Lived Old Mother Mole and her little moles nine.
"Burrow," said their mother. "We burrow," said the nine.
So they burrowed all day near the loblolly pine.

Over in the meadow in a cozy pig pen,
Lived Old Mother Pig and her little piglets ten.
"Squeal," said their mother. "We squeal," said the ten.
So they squealed all day in their cozy pig pen.

Over in the meadow in the soft summer heaven,
Lived Old Mother Firefly and her little flies eleven.
"Shine," said their mother. "We shine," said the eleven.
So they shone like stars in the soft summer heaven.

Over in the meadow where the river banks shelve,
Lived Old Mother Beaver and her little beavers twelve.
"Gnaw," said their mother. "We gnaw," said the twelve.
So they gnawed all day where the river banks shelve.

Hurry, Little Pony

Spanish Folk Song

Hurry, little pony, to the town we go.
Hurry, little pony, not too fast or slow.
One, two, three, four, five, six, seven, eight
Pony, pony, you are great!

Hurry, little pony, back to home we go.
Hurry, little pony, not too fast or slow.
One, two, three, four, five, six, seven, eight
Pony, pony, you are great!

¡Arré caballito! Vamos a Belén.
Que mañana es fiesta y pasado también.
Uno, dos, tres, cuatro, cinco, seis, siete, ocho.
¡Arré caballito! Usted me gusta mucho.

Hurry, Little Pony

Spanish Folk Song

G

1. Hur - ry, lit - tle po - ny, to the town we go.

G   **D7**

Hur - ry, lit - tle po - ny, not too fast or slow.

(for verses 1 and 2)

One, two, three, four, five, six, sev - en, eight
Po - ny, po - ny, you are great!_____

(for verses3)

U - no, dos, tres, cua - tro, cin - co, seis, si - e - te, o - cho.

Ar - ré ca - ba - lli - to Us - ted me gus - ta mu - cho.

THIS OLD MAN

English Folk Song

This old man, he played **ONE**,
He played nick-nack on my drum.
With a nick-nack, paddy whack,
give a dog a bone,
This old man came rolling home.

This old man, he played **TWO**,
He played nick-nack on my shoe.

This old man, he played **THREE**,
He played nick-nack on my tree.

This old man, he played **FOUR**,
He played nick-nack on my door.

This old man, he played **FIVE**,
He played nick-nack on my hive.

This old man, he played **SIX**,
He played nick-nack on my sticks.

This old man, he played **SEVEN**,
He played nick-nack on my oven.

This old man, he played **EIGHT**,
He played nick-nack on my gate.

This old man, he played **NINE**,
He played nick-nack on my line.

This old man, he played **TEN**,
He played nick-nack on my hen.

FIDO

The Black Pebble

by James Reeves

There went three children down to the shore
    Down to the shore and back;
There was skipping Susan and bright-eyed Sam
    And little scowling Jack.

Susan found a white cockle-shell,
    The prettiest ever seen,
And Sam picked up a piece of glass
    Rounded and smooth and green.

But Jack found only a plain black pebble
    That lay by the rolling sea,
And that was all that ever he found;
    So back they went all three.

The cockle-shell they put on the table,
    The green glass on the shelf,
But the little black pebble that Jack had found
    He kept it for himself.

Counting Petals

by Aileen Fisher

Somehow, flowers
have learned the trick
of practicing arithmetic:

Easter lilies
don't count far —
one, two, three their petals are.

Yellow poppies
count one more.
Roses count to one plus four.

How did dandelions
and such
ever learn to count so *much*?

In the Cupboard

by Barbara Ireson

I went to the cupboard

And what did I see?

One lemon

Two oranges

Three apples

Four pears

Five peaches

Six plums

Seven bananas

Eight cherries

Nine gooseberries

Ten raspberries

And up on a shelf

All by itself

A birthday cake for me.

A Few Is Not So Many

by Ruth I. Dowell

A few is not so many

And more is more than some;

But if you've got the most, you've got

A lotta bubble gum!

A few is not so many

And more is more than some,

But if you've got the most, you've got

A lotta bubble gum!

Oliver Twist

Traditional

Oliver-Oliver-Oliver Twist

Bet you a penny you can't do this:

Number ONE — touch your tongue

Number TWO — touch your shoe

Number THREE — touch your knee

Number FOUR — touch the floor

Number FIVE — look alive

Number SIX — wiggle your hips

Number SEVEN — jump to Heaven

Number EIGHT — stand up straight

Number NINE — walk the line

Number TEN — start again.

The Very Nicest Place

Anonymous

The fish lives in the brook,
The bird lives in the tree,
But home's the very nicest place
For a little child like me.

Every Time I Climb a Tree

by David McCord

Every time I climb a tree
Every time I climb a tree
Every time I climb a tree
I scrape a leg
Or skin a knee
And every time I climb a tree
I find some ants
Or dodge a bee
And get the ants
All over me

And every time I climb a tree
Where have you been?
They say to me
But don't they know that I am free
Every time I climb a tree?
I like it best
To spot a nest
That has an egg
or maybe three

And then I skin
The other leg
But every time I climb a tree
I see a lot of things to see
Swallows rooftops and TV
And all the fields and farms there be
Every time I climb a tree
Though climbing may be good for ants
It isn't awfully good for pants
But still it's pretty good for me
Every time I climb a tree

Fishes' Evening Song

by Dahlov Ipcar

Flip flop,
Flip flap,
Slip slap,
Lip lap;
Water sounds,
Soothing sounds.
We fan our fins
As we lie
Resting here
Eye to eye.
Water falls
Drop by drop,
Plip plop,
Plink plunk,
Splish splash;
Fish fins fan,
Fish tails swish,
Swush, swash, swish.
This we wish …
Water cold,
Water clear,
Water smooth,
Just to soothe
Sleepy fish.

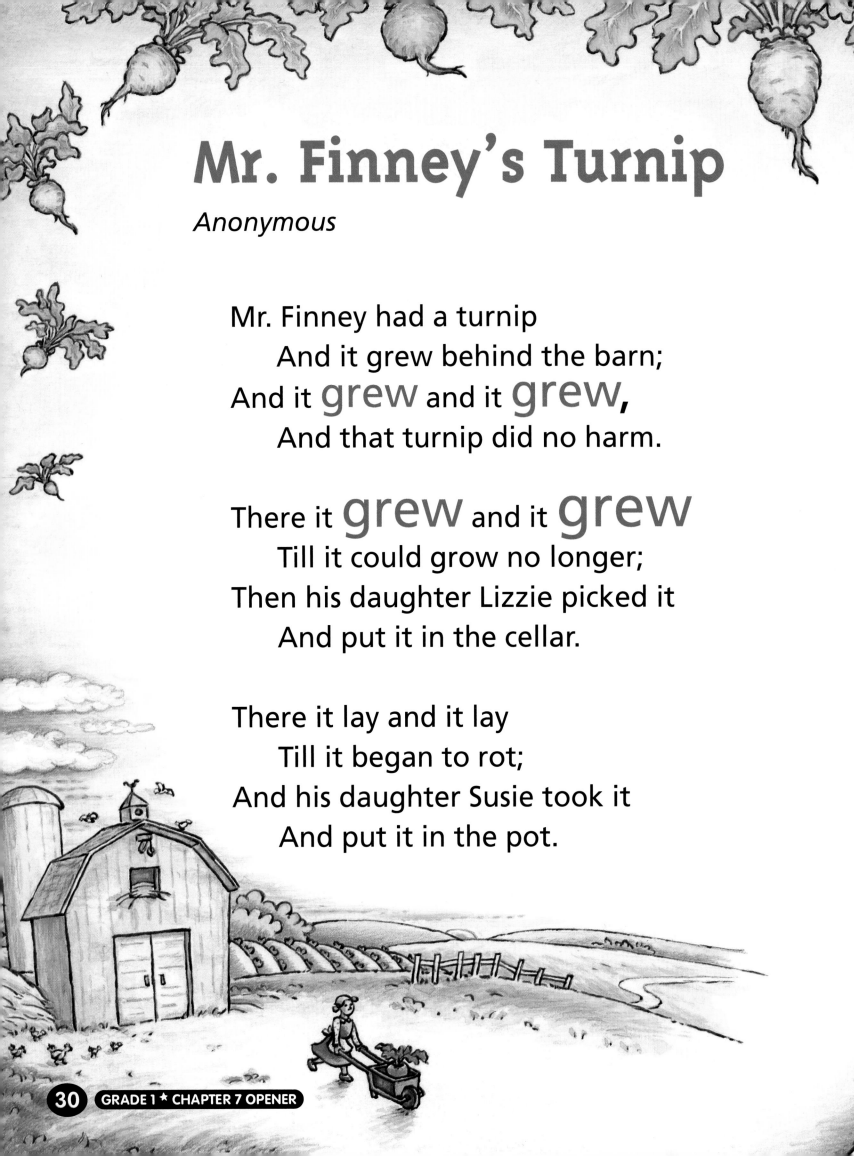

Mr. Finney's Turnip

Anonymous

Mr. Finney had a turnip
    And it grew behind the barn;
And it grew and it grew,
    And that turnip did no harm.

There it grew and it grew
    Till it could grow no longer;
Then his daughter Lizzie picked it
    And put it in the cellar.

There it lay and it lay
    Till it began to rot;
And his daughter Susie took it
    And put it in the pot.

And they boiled it and boiled it
    As long as they were able;
And then his daughters took it
    And put it on the table.

Mr. Finney and his wife
    They sat them down to sup;
And they ate and they ate
    And they ate that turnip up.

Jump or Jiggle

by Evelyn Beyer

Frogs jump
Caterpillars hump

Worms wiggle
Bugs jiggle

Rabbits hop
Horses clop

Snakes slide
Sea gulls glide

Mice creep
Deer leap

Puppies bounce
Kittens pounce

Lions stalk —
But —
I walk!

We're Racing, Racing Down the Walk

by Phyllis McGinley

We're racing, racing down the walk,

Over the pavement and round the block.

We rumble along till the sidewalk ends —

Felicia and I and half our friends.

Our hair flies backward. It's whish and whirr!

She roars at me and I shout at her

As past the porches and garden gates

We rattle and rock

On our roller skates.

Barney Has a Basketball

by Ruth I. Dowell

Barney has a basketball.
It's red and white and blue;
And, if you play the game with him,
He'll pass the ball to you.

You catch it and you dribble,
And you run and put it in.
"That's 'two' for us and 'none' for them:
I think we're gonna win!"

BEHIND THE MUSEUM DOOR

by Lee Bennett Hopkins

What's behind the museum door?

Ancient necklaces,
African art,
Armor of knights,
A peasant cart;

Pioneer wagons,
Vintage cars,
A planetarium

ceilinged

with stars;

Priceless old coins,
A king's golden throne,
Mummies in linen,

And

A dinosaur bone.

Jenny the Juvenile Juggler

by Dennis Lee

Jenny had hoops she could sling in the air
And she brought them along to the Summerhill Fair.
And a man from a carnival sideshow was there,
Who declared that he needed a juggler.

And it's

    Oops! Jenny, whoops! Jenny,

    Swing along your hoops, Jenny,

    Spin a little pattern as you go;

Because it's

    Oops! Jenny's hoops! Jenny,

    Sling a loop-the-loop, Jenny,

    Whoops! Jenny, oops! Jenny, O!

Well, the man was astonished at how the hoops flew,
And he said, "It's amazing what some kids can do!"
And now at the carnival, Act Number Two
Is Jenny the Juvenile Juggler.

And it's
    Oops! Jenny, whoops! Jenny,
    Swing along your hoops, Jenny,
    Spin a little pattern as you go;
Because it's
    Oops! Jenny's hoops! Jenny,
    Sling a loop-the-loop, Jenny,
    Whoops! Jenny, oops! Jenny, O!

Valentines

by Aileen Fisher

I gave a hundred Valentines.
A hundred, did I say?
I gave a *thousand* Valentines
one cold and wintry day.

I didn't put my name on them
or any other words,
because my Valentines were seeds
for February birds.

BRACHIOSAURUS

by Mary Ann Hoberman

This dinosaur is now extinct
While I am still extant.
I'd like to bring it back alive.
  (Unhappily I can't.)
The largest ones weighed fifty tons
And stood three stories high.
Their dinner ration? Vegetation.
  (Never hurt a fly.)
Alas! Alack! They're dead and gone
Through failure to adapt
And only known by track and bone.
  (I wish we'd overlapped.)

Follow the Leader
by Harry Behn

Follow the leader away in a row,

Into the barn and out we go,

A long slide down the hay,

Splash in a puddle, through a hedge,

And slowly up to the buzzing edge

Of a bees' hive, then run away!

Oh what a wonderful game to play!

Follow the leader on and on,

Around a tree, across a lawn,

Under the sprinkler's drifting spray,

Eat one berry, let two drop,

A somersault and a hippity-hop!

Oh what a wonderful game to play!

All over the farm on a summer day!

Ten Potatoes in a Pot

Traditional

TEN potatoes in a pot,

Take two out and eight stay hot.

EIGHT potatoes in the pan,

Take two out, there's six to plan.

SIX potatoes on the stove,

Take two off and four's the trove.

FOUR potatoes in the kettle,

Take two out, leave two to settle.

TWO potatoes still aboil,

Take them out before they spoil.

Chook Chook Chook

Traditional

Chook, chook, chook, chook, chook,
Good morning Mrs. Hen.
How many chickens have you got?
Madam, I've got ten.
Four of them are yellow,
And four of them are brown,
And two of them are speckled red,
The nicest in the town.

Kittens

Traditional

Five little kittens
Sleeping on a chair.
One rolled off,
Leaving four there.

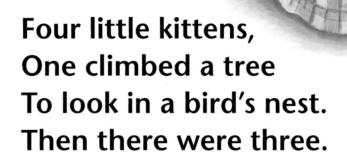

Four little kittens,
One climbed a tree
To look in a bird's nest.
Then there were three.

Three little kittens
Wondered what to do.
One saw a mouse.
Then there were two.

Two little kittens
Playing near a wall.
One little kitten
Chased a red ball.

One little kitten
With fur soft as silk,
Left all alone
To drink a dish of milk.

Ten Puppies · *Diez perritos*

Puerto Rican Folk Song

1 Oh, I used to have ten puppies,
Oh, I used to have ten puppies;
One fell in the snow so fine,
Leaving me with only nine.

Yo tenía diez perritos,
Yo tenía diez perritos;
Uno se cayó en la nieve
ya no más me quedan nueve.

2 Oh, I used to have nine puppies,
Oh, I used to have nine puppies;
One went running through the gate,
Leaving me with only eight.

...eight... One went flying up to heaven, ...seven.

...seven...One went running after sticks, ...six.

...six... One went out to take a drive, ...five.

...five... One was left outside the door, ...four.

...four... One was barking at a tree, ...three.

...three...One was chewing on a shoe, ...two.

...two... One went running just for fun, ...one.

...one... One went chasing a brown cow,
So I have no puppy now.

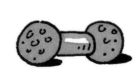

Ten Puppies *Diez perritos*

Puerto Rican Folk Song

F   B♭   F

1. Oh, I used to have ten pup - pies, Oh, I
Yo te - ní - a diez pe - rri - tos, Yo te -
yō te nē' ä dyes pe rē' tōs yō te

B♭   F

used to have ten pup - pies, One fell
ní - a diez pe - rri - tos, U - no
nē' ä dyes pe rē' tōs ōo' nō

C7   F

in the snow so fine, Leav-ing
se ca yó en la nie - ve ya - no
sä kä yō'en lä nye' ve yä nō

C7   F

me with on - ly nine.
mas me que dan nue - ve.
mäs mā kā' dän nōoe' ve

NINE BLACK CATS

by Dennis Lee

As I went up
To Halifax,
I met a man
With nine black cats.

ONE was tubby,
TWO was thin,
THREE had a pimple
On his chin-chin-chin;

FOUR ate pizza,
FIVE ate lox,
SIX ate the wool
From her long black socks;

SEVEN had a dory,
EIGHT had a car,
And NINE sang a song
On a steel guitar.

So tell me true
When you hear these facts —
How many were going
To Halifax?

Keziah

by Gwendolyn Brooks

I have a secret place to go.
Not anyone may know.

And sometimes when the wind is rough
I cannot get there fast enough.

And sometimes when my mother
Is scolding my big brother,

My secret place, it seems to me,
Is quite the only place to be.

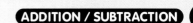

Addition

from *Take a Number*
by *Mary O'Neill*

Addition means more
Than we had before.
Addition is when company comes,
Or the recipe says: "Add flour."
Or you've grown an inch, and now you're allowed
To stay up an extra hour.

Subtraction

from *Take a Number*
by Mary O'Neill

Subtraction means that when it's finished
What you had has been diminished.

Subtraction is to lose a tooth,
Shed five pounds, cut your hair,
Miss a lesson, shrink a shirt,
Smash a toy beyond repair.

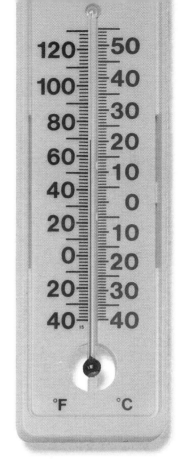

Eight Pigs

by Liz Cromwell and Dixie Hibner

Two mother pigs lived in a pen,

Each had four babies and that made ten.

These four babies were black and white.

These four babies were black as night.

All eight babies loved to play.

And they rolled and they rolled in the mud all day.

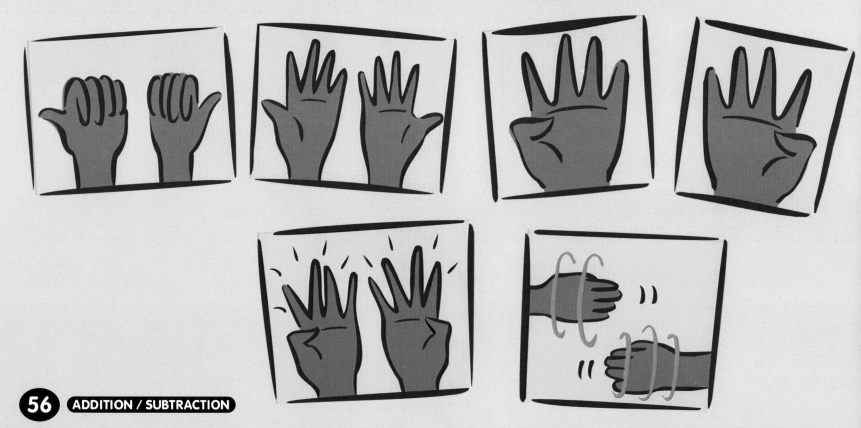

There Were Two Wrens

Traditional

There were two wrens upon a tree.
Whistle and I'll come to thee.
Another came, and there were three.
Whistle and I'll come to thee.
Another came and there were four.
You needn't whistle anymore.
For being frightened, off they flew.
And there are none to show to you.

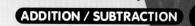

Wishes

Anonymous

Said the first little chicken
With a queer little squirm,
"I wish I could find
A fat little worm."

Said the second little chicken
With an odd little shrug,
"I wish I could find
A fat little slug."

Said the third little chicken
With a sharp little squeal,
"I wish I could find
Some nice yellow meal!"

Said the fourth little chicken
With a small sigh of grief,
"I wish I could find
A little green leaf."

Said the fifth little chicken
With a faint little moan,
"I wish I could find
A small gravel stone."

"Now see here," said their mother
From the green garden patch.
"If you want any breakfast,
Just come here and
            SCRATCH!"

TOMMY

by Gwendolyn Brooks

I put a seed into the ground

And said, "I'll watch it grow."

I watered it and cared for it

As well as I could know.

One day I walked in my back yard,

And oh, what did I see!

My seed had popped itself right out,

Without consulting me.

My Teddy Bear

by Margaret Hillert

A teddy bear is nice to hold.

The one I have is getting old.

His paws are almost wearing out

And so's his funny furry snout

From rubbing on my nose of skin,

And all his fur is pretty thin.

A ribbon and a piece of string

Make a sort of necktie thing.

His eyes came out and now instead

He has some new ones made of thread.

I take him everywhere I go

And tell him all the things I know.

I like the way he feels at night,

All snuggled up against me tight.

Bugs

by Margaret Wise Brown

I like bugs.
Black bugs,
Green bugs,
Bad bugs,
Mean bugs,
Any kind of bug,

A bug in a rug,
A bug in the grass,
A bug on the sidewalk,
A bug in a glass —
I like bugs.

Round bugs,
Shiny bugs,
Fat bugs,
Buggy bugs,
Big bugs,
Ladybugs,
I like bugs.

Space Walk

by Katherine Mead

If I could walk in outer space
I think that I would love that place!
With fat, round moons and shooting stars
And Mercury, Venus, Pluto, and Mars.

I'd dress up in a shiny suit
Put on my helmet and my boots.
I'd not forget my telephone
So I could call my mom at home.

I'd call her from a shooting star,
To tell her just how very far
The asteroids and planets fly
Above the earth as it zips by.

I'd slide along the Milky Way
And watch the night turn into day.
I'd wave at folks in my hometown
And watch the earth from upside down.

If I could walk in outer space
I *know* that I would love that place!
And even better it would be
If you could come along with me.

THE ANTS AT THE OLYMPICS

by Richard Digance

At last year's Jungle Olympics,
the Ants were completely outclassed.
In fact, from an entry of sixty-two teams,
the Ants came their usual last.

They didn't win one single medal.
Not that that's a surprise.
The reason was not lack of trying,
but more their unfortunate size.

While the cheetahs won most of the sprinting
and the hippos won putting the shot,
the Ants tried sprinting but couldn't,
and tried to put but could not.

It was sad for the Ants 'cause they're sloggers.
They turn out for every event.
With their shorts and their bright orange tee-shirts,
their athletes are proud they are sent.

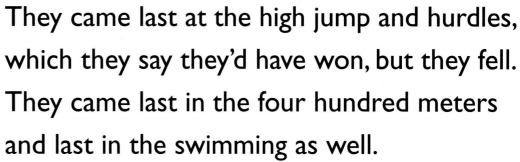

They came last at the high jump and hurdles,
which they say they'd have won, but they fell.
They came last in the four hundred meters
and last in the swimming as well.

They came last in the long-distance running,
though they say they might have come first.
And they might if the other sixty-one teams
hadn't put in a finishing burst.

But each year they turn up regardless.
They're popular in the parade.
The other teams whistle and cheer them,
aware of the journey they've made.

For the Jungle Olympics in August,
they have to set off New Year's Day.
They didn't arrive the year before last.
They set off but went the wrong way.

So long as they try there's a reason.
After all, it's only a sport.
They'll be back next year to bring up the rear,
and that's an encouraging thought.

1 2 3 4 5 6 7 8 9 10 11 12 13 14 15 16 17 18 19 20 21 22 23 24 25 26 27 28 29 30 31 32

Centipede

by David McCord

This centipede has fifty legs
and fifty others which are pegs.
The tragedy occurred on ice:
he slipped, lost fifty in a trice.
And since no trace of trice was found,
he barely managed on the ground
with half his legs not under him;
but could no longer on a limb
have fifty back legs firmly there
against the bark, as in the air
he'd wave the other fifty. You've
seen how he does it. You approve
of fifty peg legs for this chap?
Some people wouldn't give a rap.

Locust

by Mary Ann Hoberman

One locust alone doesn't make any trouble.

The same thing is true when the locusts are double.

Three locusts are lovely.

Four locusts are sweet.

Five locusts collected do not overeat.

Six locusts, one locust, cause little complaint,

While seven assembled show equal restraint.

Eight locusts located together are fine.

It's equally fine when their number is nine.

Ten locusts dine lightly wherever they dine.

A dozen?

A hundred?

A thousand?

It's strange;

But when they feel crowded, they totally change.

Ten thousand?

A million?

The figure grows bigger;

But how many locusts are needed to trigger

That change in complexion, behavior, and mood

That changes the way that they feel about food?

One locust alone simply nibbles and stops;

But locusts in crowds chew up all of the crops.

How Do You Make a Pizza Grow?

by Eve Merriam

How do you make a pizza grow?

You pound and you pull and you stretch the dough
And throw in tomatoes and oregano.

Pizza platter for twenty-two,
Pour on the oil and soak it through.

Pizza slices for forty-four,
Chop up onions, make some more.

Pizza pie for sixty-six
With mozzarella cheese that melts and sticks.

Pizza pizza for ninety-nine
With pepperoni sausage ground-up fine.

Pizza pizza stretch the dough,
Pizza pizza make it grow.

Feet

by Aileen Fisher

Feet of snails
are only one.
Birds grow two
to hop and run.
Dogs and cats
and cows grow four.
Ants and beetles
add two more.
Spiders run around
on eight,
which may seem
a lot, but wait —
Centipedes
have more than *thirty*
feet to wash
when they get dirty.

CHARLEY NEEDS A HAIRCUT

by Ruth I. Dowell

Charley needs a haircut — doesn't wanna go,

Even though the barber has three chairs in a row:

One for Charley's father,

One for Brother Ken,

Another chair for Charley.

Will he go or has he been?

Sing a Song of People

by Lois Lenski

Sing a song of people
   Walking fast or slow;
People in the city,
   Up and down they go.

   People on the sidewalk,
   People on the bus;
   People passing, passing,
   In back and front of us.
   People on the subway
   Underneath the ground;
   People riding taxis
   Round and round and round.

People with their hats on,
Going in the doors;
People with umbrellas
When it rains and pours.
People in tall buildings
And in stores below;
Riding elevators
Up and down they go.

People walking singly,
People in a crowd;
People saying nothing,
People talking loud.
People laughing, smiling,
Grumpy people too;
People who just hurry
And never look at you!

Sing a song of people
    Who like to come and go;
Sing of city people
    You see but never know!

A Diller a Dollar

Mother Goose

A diller, a dollar, a ten o'clock scholar!

What makes you come so soon?

You used to come at ten o'clock,

But now you come at noon.

Wee Willie Winkie

Mother Goose

Wee Willie Winkie
 runs through the town,
Upstairs and downstairs,
 in his nightgown;
Rapping at the window,
 crying through the lock,
"Are the children in their beds?
 Now it's eight o'clock."

MINNIE

by Ruth I. Dowell

Minnie spent her money on a frozen lemon-lime.

Now she hasn't any — not a penny, not a dime!

"Better save your money, Minnie, maybe you should try:

There will be another day with other things to buy!"

Mr. Tickle Lickle

by Ruth I. Dowell

Mr. Tickle Lickle bought a feather for a nickel

And he stuck it in the middle of his hat.

    (TWEET! TWEET!)

Now, he's singing like a bird — like a bird you never heard!

And he only paid a nickel! Think of that!

    (SOME HAT!)

Bedtime

by Eleanor Farjeon

Five minutes, five minutes more, please!
    Let me stay five minutes more!
Can't I just finish the castle
    I'm building here on the floor?
Can't I just finish the story
    I'm reading here in my book?
Can't I just finish this bead-chain —
    It *almost* is finished, look!
Can't I just finish this game, please?
    When a game's once begun
It's a pity never to find out
    Whether you've lost or won.
Can't I just stay five minutes?
    Well, can't I stay just four?
Three minutes, then? two minutes?
    Can't I stay *one* minute more?

IF I ONLY HAD A NICKEL

by Ruth I. Dowell

If I only had a nickel
I would buy myself a pickle
And I'd put it in the middle
Of a sandwich with a little
Bit of butter and baloney
And I'd eat it, if I only
Had a nickel
For a pickle —
But I don't!

Little Old Lady

by Ruth I. Dowell

Little old lady, I like your new hat!

Where did you pick up a beauty like that?

"I bought it," she said, "at a neighborhood sale

For twenty-five cents and a ten-penny nail!"

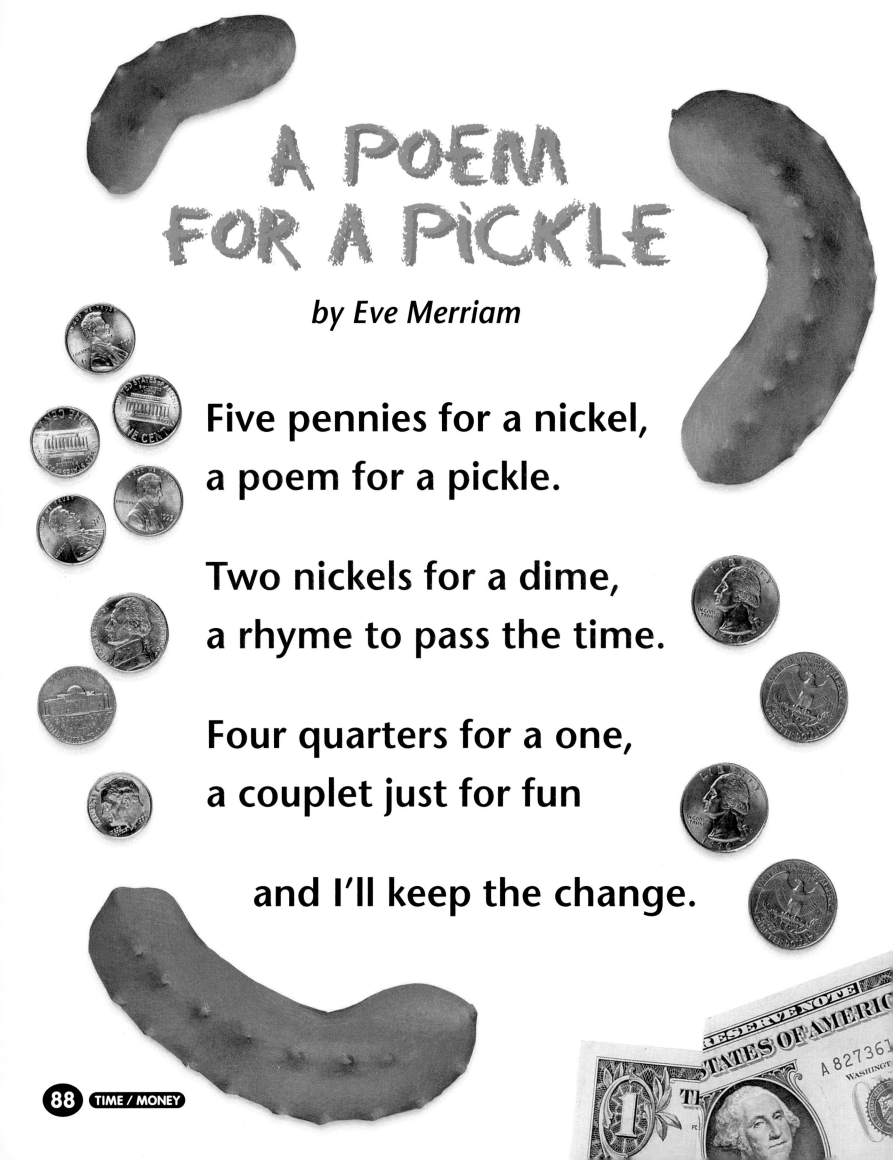

A POEM FOR A PICKLE

by Eve Merriam

Five pennies for a nickel,
a poem for a pickle.

Two nickels for a dime,
a rhyme to pass the time.

Four quarters for a one,
a couplet just for fun

and I'll keep the change.

POP! GOES THE WEASEL

American Singing Game

A penny for a spool of thread,
A penny for a needle.
That's the way the money goes,
Pop! goes the weasel.

Dangerous

by Dorothy Aldis

When we're
Hunting
We explore
Squares upon the
kitchen floor;

We must
Get from
Here to there
Without touching
Anywhere;
For this
Square is
Safe for us.
But that one is
Dangerous.

Skyscrapers

by Rachel Field

Do skyscrapers ever grow tired
Of holding themselves up high?
Do they ever shiver on frosty nights
With their tops against the sky?
Do they feel lonely sometimes
Because they have grown so tall?
Do they ever wish they could lie right down
And never get up at all?

Four Shapes

by Katherine Mead

What is a circle?

A Harvest moon,
A fat balloon,
A dinner plate,
The donut you ate.

The face of a clock,
Some chicken pox,
A tiny gold ring,
Your mouth when you sing.

What is a square?

Some buttons on coats,
Some cards and some notes,
A picture frame,
A place for a name.

One side of a box,
The shape of some blocks,
A part of a door,
The tiles on the floor.

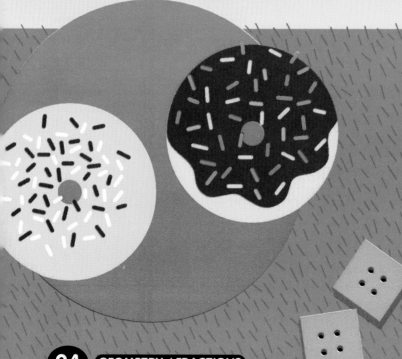

What is a triangle?

The roof of a house,
The ear of a mouse,
The top of an A
When you print a neat way.

The nose of a cat,
An old soldier's hat,
An instrument made
For a rhythm parade.

What is a rectangle?

A tall wooden door,
The boards on the floor,
A sign on the street,
A block of concrete.

One car of a train,
A window pane,
A box for a shoe,
A picture of you.

ANIMALS' HOUSES

by James Reeves

Of animals' houses
    Two sorts are found –
Those which are square ones
    And those which are round.

Square is a hen-house,
    A kennel, a sty:
Cows have square houses
    And so have I.

A snail's shell is curly,
    A bird's nest round;
Rabbits have twisty burrows
    Underground.

But the fish in the bowl
    And the fish at sea –
Their houses are round
    As a house can be.

CIRCLES
by Harry Behn

The things to draw with compasses

Are suns and moons and circleses

And rows of humptydumpasses

Or anything in circuses

Like hippopotamusseses

And hoops and camels' humpasses

And wheels on clownses busseses

And fat old elephumpasses.

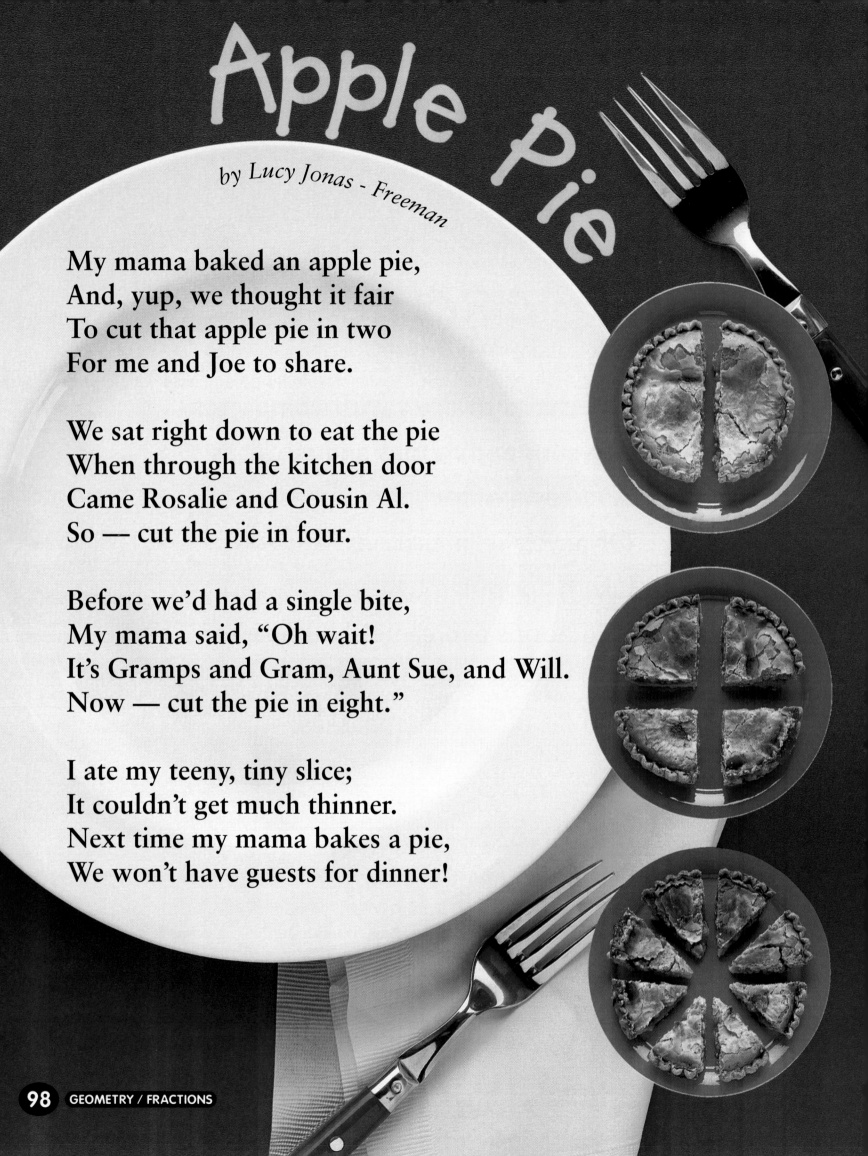

Apple Pie

by *Lucy Jonas - Freeman*

My mama baked an apple pie,
And, yup, we thought it fair
To cut that apple pie in two
For me and Joe to share.

We sat right down to eat the pie
When through the kitchen door
Came Rosalie and Cousin Al.
So — cut the pie in four.

Before we'd had a single bite,
My mama said, "Oh wait!
It's Gramps and Gram, Aunt Sue, and Will.
Now — cut the pie in eight."

I ate my teeny, tiny slice;
It couldn't get much thinner.
Next time my mama bakes a pie,
We won't have guests for dinner!

SHAPES

by Shel Silverstein

A square was sitting quietly
Outside his rectangular shack
When a triangle came down – kerplunk! –
And struck him in the back.
"I must go to the hospital,"
Cried the wounded square,
So a passing rolling circle
Picked him up and took him there.

Yesterday's Paper

by Mabel Watts

Yesterday's paper makes a hat,

Or a boat,

Or a plane,

Or a playhouse mat.

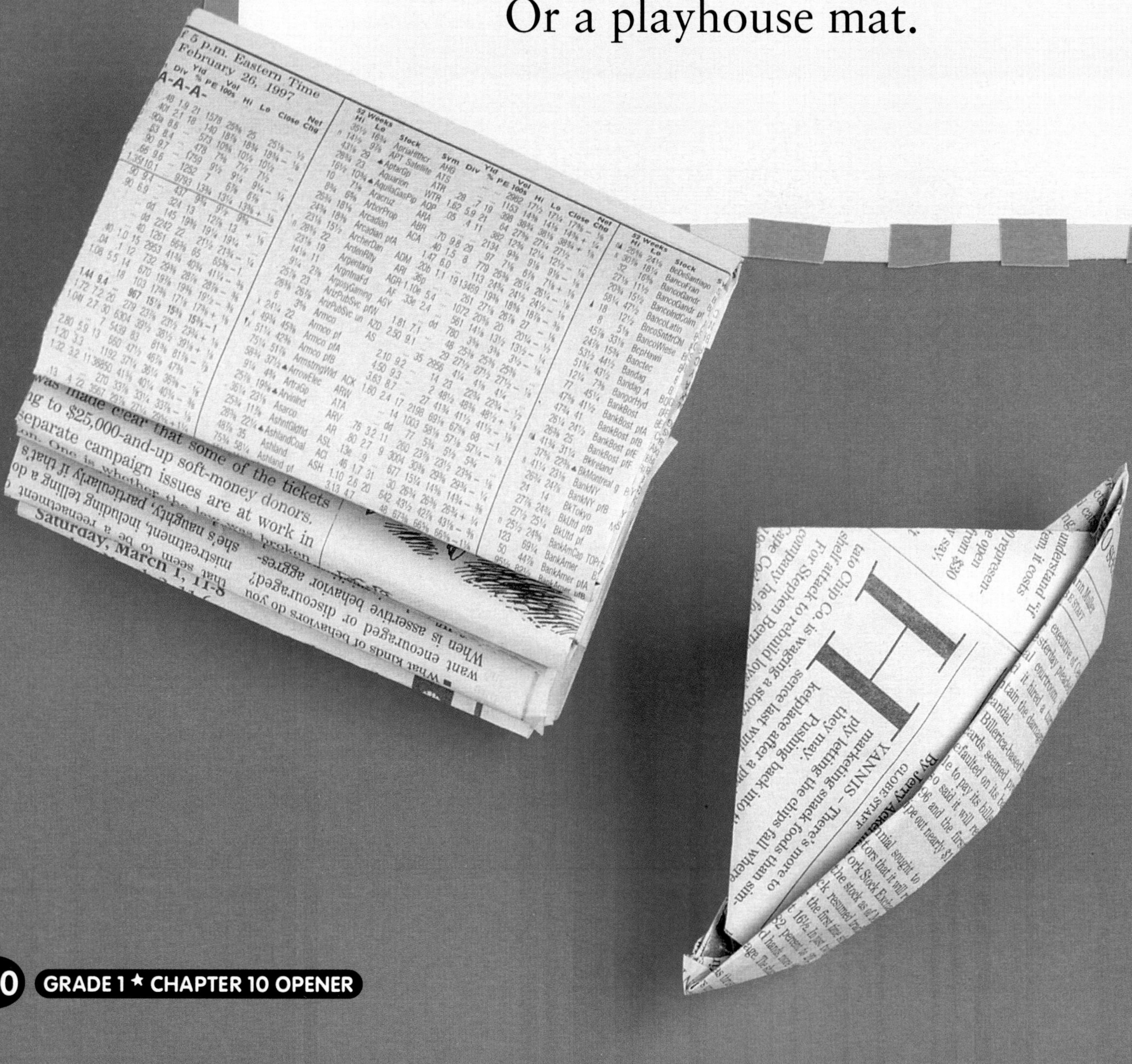

Yesterday's paper makes things

Like that –

And a very fine tent

For a sleeping cat.

Just Watch

by Myra Cohn Livingston

Watch

    how high

    I'm jumping,

Watch

    how far

    I hop,

Watch

    how long

    I'm skipping,

Watch

    how fast

    I stop!

ONE INCH TALL

by Shel Silverstein

If you were only one inch tall, you'd ride a worm to school.

The teardrop of a crying ant would be your swimming pool.

A crumb of cake would be a feast

And last you seven days at least,

A flea would be a frightening beast

If you were one inch tall.

If you were only one inch tall, you'd walk beneath the door,

And it would take about a month to get down to the store.

A bit of fluff would be your bed,

You'd swing upon a spider's thread,

And wear a thimble on your head

If you were one inch tall.

You'd surf across the kitchen sink upon a stick of gum.

You couldn't hug your mama, you'd just have to hug her thumb.

You'd run from people's feet in fright,

To move a pen would take all night,

(This poem took fourteen years to write—

'Cause I'm just one inch tall).

Inchworm

by N. M. Bodecker

An inchworm
walked
a bit
of string,
and as
she walked
I heard
her sing

a song
of measured
joy
and sense
(each sings
her
own
experience).

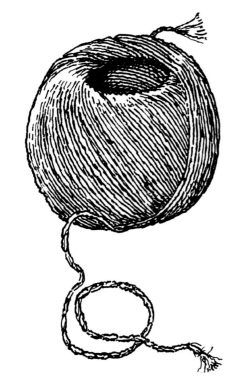

And this
was her
contented
song:
"Today
was nineteen
inches
long."

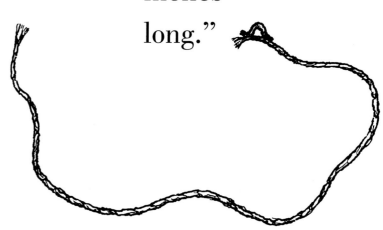

EAST AND WEST

by Liz Cromwell and Dixie Hibner

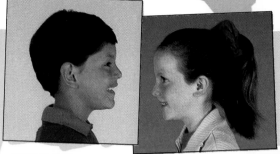

This is **EAST**, and this is **WEST**.
Soon I'll learn to say the rest.

This is **HIGH** and this is **LOW**,
Only to see how much I know.

This is **NARROW**, and this is **WIDE**.
See how much I know beside.

DOWN is where my feet you see,
UP is where my head should be.

Here is my nose, and there are my eyes.
Don't you think I'm getting wise?

Now my eyes will **OPEN** keep
I **SHUT** them when I go to sleep.

two friends

by Nikki Giovanni

lydia and shirley have

two pierced ears and

two bare ones

five pigtails

two pairs of sneakers

two berets

two smiles

one necklace

one bracelet

lots of stripes and

one good friendship

Mr. Bidery's Spidery Garden
by David McCord

Poor old Mr. Bidery.

His garden's awfully spidery;

Bugs use it as a hidery.

In April it was seedery,

By May a mass of weedery;

And oh, the bugs! How greedery.

White flowers out or buddery,

Potatoes made it spuddery,

And when it rained, what muddery!

June days grow long and shaddery;

Bullfrog forgets his taddery;

The spider legs his laddery.

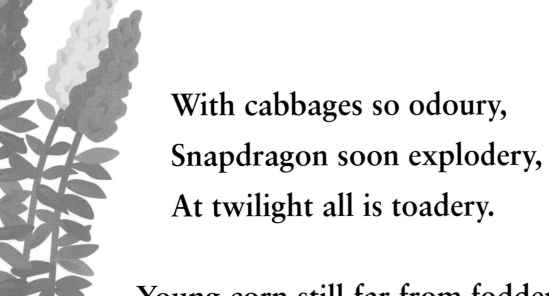

With cabbages so odoury,

Snapdragon soon explodery,

At twilight all is toadery.

Young corn still far from foddery

No sign of goldenrodery,

Yet feeling low and doddery.

Is poor old Mr. Bidery,

His garden lush and spidery,

His apples green, not cidery.

Pea-picking is so poddery!

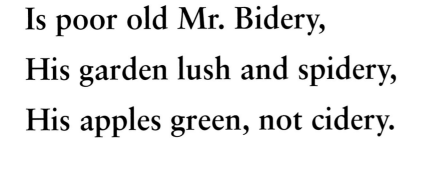

The Ants Go Marching One by One

Traditional

The ants go marching ONE by ONE,
Hurrah! Hurrah!
The ants go marching ONE by ONE,
Hurrah! Hurrah!
The ants go marching ONE by ONE,
And the last one stops to have some fun.
And they all go marching
Down and around
And into the ground
To get out of the rain.
BOOM, BOOM, BOOM, BOOM,
BOOM, BOOM, BOOM.

The ants go marching TWO by TWO,
Hurrah! Hurrah!
The ants go marching TWO by TWO,
Hurrah! Hurrah!
The ants go marching TWO by TWO,
And the last one stops to tie his shoe,
And they all go marching
Down and around
And into the ground
To get out of the rain.
BOOM, BOOM, BOOM, BOOM,
BOOM, BOOM, BOOM.

The ants go marching THREE by THREE,
And the last one stops to climb a tree…

The ants go marching FOUR by FOUR,
And the last one stops to close the door…

The ants go marching FIVE by FIVE,
And the last one stops to take a dive…

The ants go marching SIX by SIX,
And the last one stops to pick up sticks…

The ants go marching SEVEN by SEVEN,
And the last one stops to go to heaven…

The ants go marching EIGHT by EIGHT,
And the last one stops to shut the gate…

The ants go marching NINE by NINE,
And the last one stops and falls behind…

The ants go marching TEN by TEN,
Hurrah! Hurrah!
The ants go marching TEN by TEN,
Hurrah! Hurrah!
The ants go marching TEN by TEN,
And the last one stops and shouts, "The End!"
And they all go marching
Down and around
And into the ground
To get out of the rain.
BOOM, BOOM, BOOM, BOOM,
BOOM, BOOM, BOOM.

Old Noah's Ark

Folk Rhyme

Old Noah once he built an ark,
And patched it up with hickory bark.
He anchored it to a great big rock,
And then he began to load his stock.

The animals went in one by one,
The elephant chewing a caraway bun.

The animals went in two by two,
The crocodile and the kangaroo.

The animals went in three by three,
The tall giraffe and the tiny flea.

The animals went in four by four,
The hippopotamus stuck in the door.

The animals went in five by five,
The bees mistook the bear for a hive.

The animals went in six by six,
The monkey was up to his usual tricks.

The animals went in seven by seven,
Said the ant to the elephant, "Who are you shovin'?"

The animals went in eight by eight,
Some were early and some were late.

The animals went in nine by nine,
They all formed fours and marched in a line.

The animals went in ten by ten,
If you want any more, you can read it again.

Soda Shop

Traditional

What's your name?

Mary Jane.

Where do you live?

Down the lane.

What do you keep?

A little shop.

What do you sell?

Ginger pop.

How many bottles do you sell in a day?

Twenty-four, now go away.

25¢

DIVIDING

by David McCord

Here is an apple, ripe and red
    On one side; on the other green.
And I must cut it with a knife
    Across or in between.

And if I cut it in between,
    And give the best (as Mother said)
To you, then I must keep the green,
    And you will have the red.

But Mother says that green is tough
Unless it comes in applesauce.
You *know* what? I've been sick enough:
I'll cut it straight across.

Imagine a World

from *Take a Number*
by *Mary O'Neill*

Imagine a world
Without mathematics:
Unmeasured houses,
Cellars and attics,
Crooked doorways,
Tilted roofs,
Millions of problems
And no proofs.
No dimes or dollars,
No clocks or meters,
Thermometers or high-frequency
Tweeters;
And absolutely no way
Of knowing
How fast or slow
A thing is going.

No rulers or scales,
No inches or feet,
No dates or numbers
On house or street,
No prices or weights,
No determining heights,
No hours running through
Days and nights.
No zero, no birthdays,
No way to subtract
All of the guesswork
Surrounding the fact.
No sizes for shoes,
Or suit or hat…
Wouldn't it be awful
To live like that?

POEMS BY AUTHOR

Harry Behn

Harry Behn grew up in Prescott, in what was then the territory of Arizona. In 1947 that he moved to Connecticut to settle and write. In his lifetime, Harry Behn wrote numerous books of poetry, many with themes about nature, for children, adolescents and adults. However he wrote his first poem for children when he was fifty years old, inspired by his three-year old daughter who referred to the stars in the night sky as "moon-babies." In 1949, his first anthology for children, *The Little Hill*, (Harcourt, Brace, Jovanovich), was published. A collection of his previously published poetry for children, *Crickets and Bullfrogs and Whispers of Thunder* (Harcourt, Brace, Jovanovich) was published posthumously in 1984.

Other children's poetry collections by Harry Behn include:
All Kinds of Time. Harcourt, Brace, Jovanovich, 1950
Windy Morning. Harcourt, Brace, Jovanovich, 1953
The Wizard in the Well. Harcourt, Brace, Jovanovich, 1956
Cricket Songs. Harcourt, Brace, Jovanovich, 1964
More Cricket Songs. Harcourt, Brace, Jovanovich, 1971

Gwendolyn Brooks

Although Gwendolyn Brooks has written poetry mostly for older students and adults, she did write one book for younger readers. The poems in *Bronzeville Boys and Girls* (Harper & Row, 1956), each poem reflecting the thoughts, feelings, and experiences of a different child. Gwendolyn Brooks is the first African American woman to win the Pulitzer Prize for Poetry, awarded in 1950 for her adult anthology, *Annie Allen*.

Aileen Fisher

Aileen Fisher grew up in Michigan, in a big white house high on the banks of the Iron River, which to this day, inspires her love of living in the country. On evening in 1927, she thought of lines for a poem on her way home from her job at a Chicago placement agency. She hurriedly wrote down and later that evening, she sent poem, "Otherwise" to Child Life magazine. It was the first of her many poems to be published. Five years later, she moved back to the country, this time in Colorado, and within a year, published her first book of poems, *The Coffee-Pot Face* (McBribe Co., 1953).

Aileen Fisher's other anthologies include:
Listen, Rabbit. T.Y. Crowell, 1964
Out in the Dark and Daylight. Harper & Row, 1980.
When It Comes to Bugs. Harper & Row, 1986

Mary Ann Hoberman

Mary Ann Hoberman decided at an early age, before she knew how to write, that she wanted to be an author. She made up stories songs and poems which she recited aloud — and sometimes very loudly! As an adult, she continued to make up made up poems and stories to entertain her four children. She finally wrote and published her first book for children, *All My Shoes Come in Two's* (Little, Brown) until 1957. This successful book was followed by many others, including:
The Looking Book. Viking, 1973.
A House is A House for Me. Viking, 1978.
Mothers, Fathers, Sisters, Brothers. Joy Street Books, 1991.

Dennis Lee

Dennis Lee is a Canadian author known for his adult poetry, scholarly essays, and literary theory. He began to write and publish for children when his own children were very young. Many of his best-known poems are for young readers.

Other titles for children by Dennis Lee include:
Wiggle to the Laundromat. New Press, 1977.
Alligator Pie. Macmillan, 1974; Houghton Mifflin, 1975.
Nicholas Knock and Other People. Macmillan, 1974; Houghton Mifflin, 1977.
Garbage Delight. Macmillan, 1977.

David McCord

About with malaria at the age of two that recurred over several years kept David McCord out of school. In his solitude he explored the world of books as well as the natural world around him, fascinated by "the sight and sound and shape of everything that moved with rhythm." McCord published his first book of poetry for children, *Far and Few: Rhymes of Never Was and Always Is* (Little, Brown), in 1952, nearly 25 years after his poetry for adults first appeared. Whether his poetry speaks of nature or of nonsense, his love of language and words is evident. In 1977, he was the first recipient of the NCTE Award for Excellence in Poetry for Children.

Collections of poetry by David McCord include:
One at a Time: His Collected Poems for the Young.
    Little, Brown, 1952.
Speak Up: More Rhymes of the Never Was and Always Is.
    Little, Brown, 1980.
Take Sky. Little, Brown, 1962.
All Small. Little, Brown, 1986.
The Star in the Pail. Little, Brown, 1986.

Phyllis McGinley

Phyllis McGinley always knew she wanted to write poetry, and began rhyming words when she was six. She started her career when she was in college, selling her poems to magazines. She later worked as a teacher and in an advertising agency until she became the poetry editor for a national magazine. Her first book for children, The Horse Who Lived Upstairs (Lippencott, 1944), was based on actual horses living in a second floor stable in New York City's Greenwich Village.

Other books for children by Phyllis McGinley include:
The Year Without a Santa Claus. Lippencott, 1957.
All Around the Town. Lippencott, 1948.
The B-Book. Crowell-Collier, 1962, 1968.

Eve Merriam

When Eve Merriam decided to look for a job, she had no idea what a poet could do. She remembered that Carl Sandberg had once worked for an advertising agency, so she applied to one as well, and later worked as a fashion editor for a magazine. Yet she never abandoned her first love, poetry. In the 1960's, she published three books of poetry for children, *Catch a Little Rhyme*, (Atheneum, 1964), *It Doesn't Always Have to Rhyme*, (Atheneum, 1962), and *There is No Rhyme for Silver.* (Atheneum, 1966). Her 1978 publication, *The Birthday Cow* (Knopf), was illustrated by her son, Guy Michel.

Other poetry collections by Eve Merriam include:
Out Loud. Atheneum, 1973.
A Word or Two with You: New Rhymes for Young Readers.
    Atheneum, 1981.
Jamboree: Rhymes for All Times. Dell, 1984.
A Sky Full of Poems. Dell, 1986.

Shel Silverstein

The light verse Shel Silverstein is recognized and loved by children of all ages. He has had many careers from cartoonist, and guitar player to songwriter. In 1974, he published his anthology, *Where the Sidewalk Ends* (Harper & Row), followed by *The Light in the Attic* (Harper & Row) in 1981. In 1985, *Light* broke the record for the longest time — well over three years — that any hardcover book has been on *The New York Times* bestseller list. In 1996, Shel Silverstein published his next anthology of poetry, *Falling Up* (Harper & Row).

Other books for children by Shel Silverstein include:
A Giraffe and a Half. Harper & Row, 1964.
The Giving Tree. Harper & Row, 1964.

"If I Only Had a Nickel" from *Move Over Mother Goose* by Ruth I. Dowell. Copyright ©1987 by Ruth I. Dowell. Reprinted with permission of the publisher, Gryphon House, Inc., Beltsville, MD 20704.

"Inchworm" from *Water Pennies and Other Poems* by N. M. Bodecker, illustrated by Erik Blegvad. Text copyright ©1989 by Tumbledown Editions. Illustrations copyright ©1991 by Erik Blegvad. Reprinted with the permission of Margaret K. McElderry Books, an imprint of Simon & Schuster Children's Publishing Division.

"In the Cupboard" from *Over and Over Again* by Barbara Ireson. Reprinted by permission of the publisher, Red Fox.

"Jenny the Juvenile Juggler" by Dennis Lee from *The Ice Cream Store* (HarperCollins Publishers, Ltd., 1991). Copyright ©1991 by Dennis Lee. With permission of the author.

"Jump or Jiggle" by Evelyn Beyer from *Another Here and Now Storybook* by Lucy Sprague Mitchell. Copyright 1937 by E.P. Dutton, Inc., renewed 1965 by Lucy Sprague Mitchell. Reprinted by permission of E.P. Dutton, Inc., a division of Penguin USA.

"Just Watch" from *Whispers and Other Poems* by Myra Cohn Livingston. Copyright ©1958 by Myra Cohn Livingston. Copyright renewed 1986 by Myra Cohn Livingston. Reprinted by permission of Marian Reiner.

"Keziah" from *Bronzeville Boys and Girls* by Gwendolyn Brooks. Copyright ©1956 by Gwendolyn Brooks Blakely. Reprinted by permission of HarperCollins Publishers.

"Little Old Lady" from *Move Over Mother Goose* by Ruth I. Dowell. Copyright ©1987 by Ruth I. Dowell. Reprinted with permission of the publisher, Gryphon House, Inc., Beltsville, MD 20704.

"Locust" from *Bugs: Poems by Mary Ann Hoberman.* Copyright ©1976 by Mary Ann Hoberman. Reprinted by permission of Gina Maccoby Literary Agency.

"Minnie" from *Move Over Mother Goose* by Ruth I. Dowell. Copyright ©1987 by Ruth I. Dowell. Reprinted with permission of the publisher, Gryphon House, Inc., Beltsville, MD 20704.

"Mr. Bidery's Spidery Garden" from *For Me to Say* by David McCord. Copyright ©1972 by David McCord. By permission of Little, Brown and Company.

"Mr. Tickle Lickle" from *Move Over Mother Goose* by Ruth I. Dowell. Copyright ©1987 by Ruth I. Dowell. Reprinted with permission of the publisher, Gryphon House, Inc., Beltsville, MD 20704.

"My Teddy Bear" from *Farther Than Far* by Margaret Hillert. Copyright ©1969 by Follett Publishing Company. Used by permission of the author who controls all rights.

"Nine Black Cats" from *The Ice Cream Store* by Dennis Lee, illustrated by David McPhail. Published in Canada by HarperCollins Publishers Ltd. and in the United States by Scholastic Inc. Copyright ©1991 by Dennis Lee. Reprinted by permission of HarperCollins Publishers Ltd. (Canada).

"One Inch Tall" from *Where the Sidewalk Ends* by Shel Silverstein. Copyright ©1974 by Evil Eye Music, Inc. Reprinted by permission of HarperCollins Publishers.

"A Poem for a Pickle" from *A Poem for a Pickle* by Eve Merriam (Morrow Jr. Books). Copyright ©1989 by Eve Merriam. Reprinted by permission of Marian Reiner.

"Shapes" from *A Light in the Attic* by Shel Silverstein. Copyright ©1981 by Evil Eye Music, Inc. Reprinted by permission of HarperCollins Publishers.

"Sing a Song of People" from *The Life I Live* by Lois Lenski. Copyright ©1965 by The Lois Lenski Covey Foundation Inc. Reprinted by permission of The Lois Lenski Covey Foundation Inc.

"Skyscrapers" from *Poems* by Rachel Field. Copyright ©1957 Macmillan Publishing Company. Reprinted with the permission of Simon & Schuster Books for Young Readers, an imprint of Simon & Schuster Children's Publishing Division.

Excerpt from *Take a Number* by Mary O'Neill. Copyright ©1968 by Mary O'Neill. Copyright renewed 1996 by Abigail Hagler and Nancy Baroni. Used by permission of Marian Reiner.

"Ten Little Froggies" from *Rhymes for Fingers and Flannelboards* by Louise Binder Scott and J. J. Thompson. Copyright ©1960 by Webster/McGraw-Hill. Reprinted by permission of T.S. Dennison Publishing.

"Tommy" from *Bronzeville Boys and Girls* by Gwendolyn Brooks. Copyright ©1956 by Gwendolyn Brooks Blakely. Reprinted by permission of HarperCollins Publishers.

"Treasure" from *Good Rhymes, Good Times* by Lee Bennett Hopkins. Copyright ©1972, 1995 by Lee Bennett Hopkins. Reprinted by permission of Curtis Brown, Ltd.

"two friends" from *Spin a Soft Black Song* by Nikki Giovanni. Text copyright ©1971, 1985 by Nikki Giovanni. Reprinted by permission of Farrar, Straus & Giroux, Inc.

"Valentines" by Aileen Fisher. By permission of the author, Aileen Fisher, who controls rights.

"We're Racing, Racing Down the Walk" from *Sugar and Spice - The ABC of Being a Girl* by Phyllis McGinley. Copyright ©1959, 1960 by Phyllis McGinley. Published by permission of Franklin Watts.

"Winter Clothes" from *A Rose on My Cake* by Karla Kuskin. Copyright ©1964 by Karla Kuskin. Reprinted by permission of the author.

"Yesterday's Paper" by Mabel Watts. Reprinted by permission of the author.

Credits

Illustration   **2-3, 114-115** Pedro Martin; **4-5, 21, 56-57** Annie Gusman; **7, 11, 15, 51** William R. Brinkley (music); **6-7, 16-17, 34-35, 46-47, 68-69, 72-73, 81, 107, 108** Darcy Schwartz; **8-9** Penny Carter; **10-11** Judith Moffatt; **12-13** Michael Jones; **14-15, 89** Holly Meade; **18-19, 62-63** Eileen Hine; **26-27** Laura DeSantis; **30-31** Enzo Giannini; **32-33** Laura Cornell; **36-37** Jim Owens; **40-41** Esther Szegedy; **44-45, 90-91** Nathan Y. Jarvis; **48-49** Pam Paparone; **50-51** Steve Henry; **52-53** Holly Berry; **58-59** Don Stuart; **60-61** Ellen Sloan Childers; **64-65** Will Terry; **66-67** Brian Lies; **70-71** Vince Andriani; **76** Raquel Sousa; **78-79** Denise & Fernando; **82-83** Jennifer Beck Harris; **84-85** René King Moreno; **94-95** Linda Davick; **96** Dorothy Donohue; **97** David Shaw; **102-103** Jennifer Plecas; **110-111** Deborah Drummond; **112-113** Andrea Barrett; **116-117** Hugh Whyte; **118-119** Cyndy Patrick; **120-121** Jack Desrocher

Assignment Photographs   **6-7, 16-17, 22-23, 54-55, 80-81, 86-87** Petrisse Briel; **10** Tony Scarpetta; **20, 24-25, 88, 100-101** Steve Nelson; **35, 72-73, 77, 98, 107, 108-109** Dorey A. Sparre **98** Karen Ahola;

Photographs   **28** Dr. Paul A. Zahl/Photo Researchers; **38** Superstock/ Royal Museum Copenhagen, Denmark (l); **38** Photo Researchers/ George Molton (tr); **39** Photo Researchers/Vanessa Vick (br); **39** Photo Researchers/ Alexander Tsiapas (l); **39** The Image Bank/ Patti McConville (tr); **43** William Johnson/Stock Boston; **55** © Peter Vandermark/Stock, Boston/ PNI; **74** Image Copyright (c) 1996 Photodisc, Inc. (t) (r); **74** Animals Animals/Patti Murray (tl); **74** The Image Bank/ Steve Grubman (bl); **75** Image Copyright (c) 1996 Photodisc, Inc. (t) (r); **75** Stock Boston/ Leonard Lee Rue (m); **75** FPG/ C.E. Lettau (bm); **92** Thierry Cariou/The Stock Market